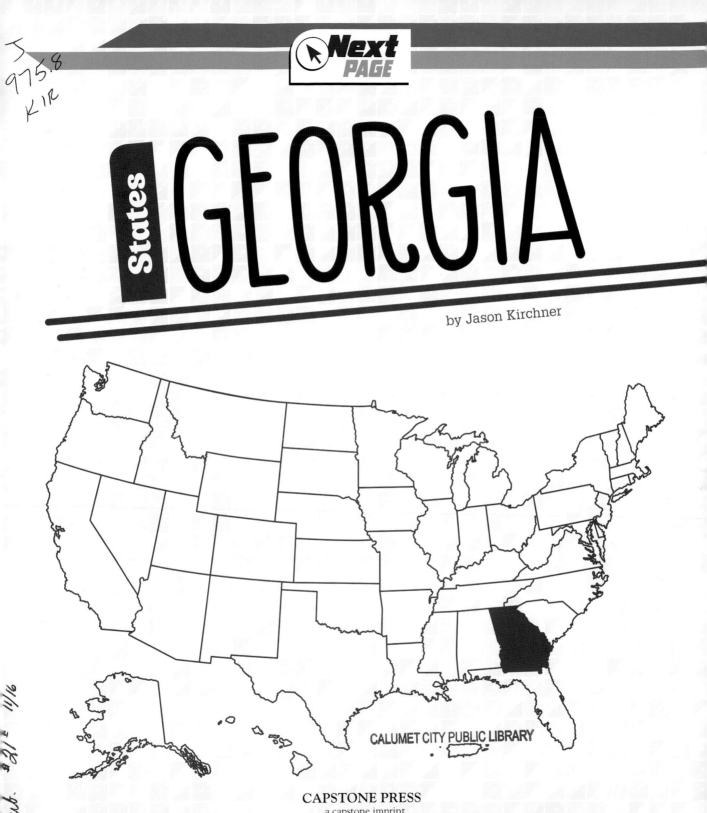

Next PAGE

States

GEORGIA

by Jason Kirchner

CAPSTONE PRESS
a capstone imprint

Next Page Books are published by Capstone Press,
1710 Roe Crest Drive, North Mankato, Minnesota 56003
www.mycapstone.com

Library of Congress Cataloging-in-Publication Data
Cataloging-in-publication information is on file with the Library of
Congress.
ISBN 978-1-5157-0396-9 (library binding)
ISBN 978-1-5157-0456-0 (paperback)
ISBN 978-1-5157-0508-6 (ebook PDF)

Editorial Credits
Jaclyn Jaycox, editor; Richard Korab and Katy LaVigne, designers;
Morgan Walters, media researcher; Laura Manthe, production specialist

Photo Credits
Capstone Press: Angi Gahler, map 4, 7; Getty Images: CNP, bottom 18,
Frank Capri, middle 19, Keystone/Stringer, bottom 19, Martin Mills, top
18; Library of Congress: Library of Congress Prints and Photographs
Division Washington, D.C., middle 18; U.S. Dept of Commerce, NOAA:
NOAA, top left 21; North Wind Picture Archives, 12; One Mile Up, Inc.,
22-23; Shutterstock: Andrew Brunk, 14, Anton Bryksin, 29, Daniel
Prudek, bottom right 21, Darryl Brooks, top left 20, Dave Newman, 13,
Everett Historical, 25, 27, f11photo, 5, Ffooter, 17, Jeffrey M. Frank,
10, JStone, top 19, kurdistan, bottom right 8, leungchopan, middle left
21, Rehan Qureshi, 15, Ritu Manoj Jethani, 9, rj lerich, top right 21,
Rob Hainer, 6, Rob Marmion, bottom 24, Ron Blanton, top right 20,
Rose Thompson, bottom right 20, Sean Pavone, 7, 16, sibyl2011, top 24,
Steve Byland, bottom left 20, Travel Bug, 11, trekandshoot, bottom left
8, Valentyn Volkov, middle right 21, Vladimir Shulenin, bottom left 21,
Waddell Images, 26, Yuri Tuchkov, cover; Wikimedia: National Archives
and Records Administration, 28

All design elements by Shutterstock

Printed and bound in China.
0316/CA21600187
012016   009436F16

TABLE OF CONTENTS

Want to take your research further? Ask your librarian if your school subscribes to PebbleGo Next. If so, when you see this helpful symbol 🖰 throughout the book, log onto www.pebblegonext.com for bonus downloads and information.

LOCATION

Georgia is the largest state east of the Mississippi River. On the southeast, Georgia touches the Atlantic Ocean. The Savannah River empties into the ocean. This river forms most of Georgia's eastern border. Just across the river is South Carolina. Tennessee and North Carolina are Georgia's northern neighbors. Florida lies along the southern border. Georgia and Florida share the Okefenokee Swamp. The Chattahoochee River forms much of Georgia's western border. Alabama lies on the other side. Atlanta is Georgia's capital and largest city. Georgia's next largest cities are Augusta, Columbus, and Savannah.

PebbleGo Next Bonus!
To print and label
your own map, go to
www.pebblegonext.com
and search keywords:

GA MAP

4

Downtown Atlanta is home to most of the city's major tourist attractions.

GEOGRAPHY

Georgia has five natural regions. These regions are the Coastal Plain, the Piedmont Plateau, the Blue Ridge, the Ridge and Valley, and the Appalachian Plateau. The Coastal Plain is a flat, lowland area. It covers about 60 percent of Georgia. Rolling hills and forests cover the Piedmont Plateau in central Georgia. Georgia's highest point is in the Blue Ridge region. Brasstown Bald rises 4,784 feet (1,458 meters) above sea level. Tall ridges and narrow valleys stretch across the Ridge and Valley region of northwestern Georgia. The Appalachian Plateau is found in Georgia's northwestern corner.

PebbleGo Next Bonus!
To watch a video about Savannah, Georgia, go to www.pebblegonext.com and search keywords:
GA VIDEO

Cloudland Canyon State Park is located in the northwest corner of Georgia. It is one of the most scenic parks in the state.

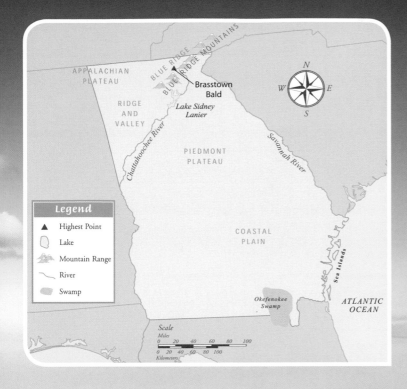

APPALACHIAN
PLATEAU

BLUE RIDGE
BLUE RIDGE MOUNTAINS

Brasstown
Bald

RIDGE
AND
VALLEY

Lake Sidney
Lanier

Chattahoochee River

PIEDMONT
PLATEAU

Savannah River

N
W   E
S

COASTAL
PLAIN

Sea Islands

Legend

▲ Highest Point
     Lake
     Mountain Range
     River
     Swamp

Okefenokee
Swamp

ATLANTIC
OCEAN

Scale
Miles
0   20   40   60   80   100
0   20   40   60   80 100
Kilometers

The Blue Ridge Mountains in
northeastern Georgia are part of
the Appalachian Mountain range.

WEATHER

Georgia has warm, sunny summers and mild winters. The average July temperature is 80 degrees Fahrenheit (27 degrees Celsius). The average January temperature is 47°F (8°C).

Average High and Low Temperatures (Atlanta, GA)

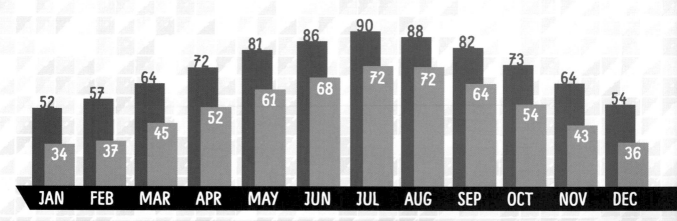

JAN	FEB	MAR	APR	MAY	JUN	JUL	AUG	SEP	OCT	NOV	DEC
52	57	64	72	81	86	90	88	82	73	64	54
34	37	45	52	61	68	72	72	64	54	43	36

LANDMARKS

Stone Mountain

Stone Mountain, east of Atlanta, is the biggest exposed mass of granite in the world. The side of the mountain has a huge sculpture of Confederate leaders carved into it. The carved area is bigger than a football field. About 4 million visitors come to the popular tourist attraction every year.

Etowah Indian Mounds

Prehistoric American Indians built the Etowah Indian Mounds. Located near Cartersville in northern Georgia, the site covers 54 acres (22 hectares) and features six earthen mounds. Visitors tour a museum filled with ancient artifacts.

Savannah Historic District

Savannah has the largest national landmark district in the country. Covering more than 20 city squares, the historic district has museums, monuments, galleries, restaurants, and historic homes and churches.

HISTORY AND GOVERNMENT

James Oglethorpe, Georgia's founder, visits the Highland colony in Georgia around 1730.

Many people lived in Georgia 2,000 years ago. They were called the Mound Builders because they built huge mounds. The Creek, Cherokee, Timucua, Yamassee, and other Indian groups later lived in Georgia. Spanish explorer Hernando de Soto arrived in 1540. Later Great Britain set up colonies in North America. James Oglethorpe started the colony of Georgia in 1732. Georgia joined other American colonies in the Revolutionary War (1775–1783). The colonists won their freedom from Great Britain in 1783. Georgia became the 4th U.S. state in 1788.

Georgia's state government has three branches. The governor is the leader of the executive branch, which carries out laws. The legislature is made up of the 56-member Senate and the 180-member House of Representatives. They make the laws for Georgia. Georgia's judges and courts are the judicial branch. They uphold the laws.

Georgia's state capitol building is located in Atlanta.

INDUSTRY

As Georgia's population has grown, so has its economy. Service industries, such as hospitals and passenger airline businesses, make up about 85 percent of the state's employment. Tourism is also an important service industry, especially in Atlanta and Savannah. Farms cover about 25 percent of Georgia's land. Poultry is the state's chief farm product. Georgia leads the nation in growing peanuts. Beef cattle, hogs, milk, cotton, tobacco, and pecans are important sources of income. Peaches are Georgia's main fruit crop.

Georgia is known for its delicious peaches, which are only available 16 weeks each year.

Manufacturing is also important to Georgia's economy. Textiles are among Georgia's top manufactured products. Georgia textiles include denim, carpet, and wool. The state also manufactures cars, airplanes, and processed foods and beverages. The major food products are baked goods, packaged chicken, and peanut butter.

Denim fabric at the final stage of the manufacturing process

POPULATION

Many Georgians descended from British, German, Austrian, and Swiss settlers. These settlers lived mainly along the coast, and many of their descendants still live in Georgia. Spanish, Portuguese, German, and Jewish settlers arrived later. Scottish and Irish people came from nearby states. Today more than 5 million white people live in Georgia. About three of every 10 Georgians are African-Americans. About 3 million African-Americans live in the state. Some have descended from former slaves. Other Georgians have Hispanic, Asian, or American Indian roots. More than 800,000 Hispanics and more than 300,000 Asians live in Georgia. American Indians make up less than 1 percent of Georgia's population.

Population by Ethnicity

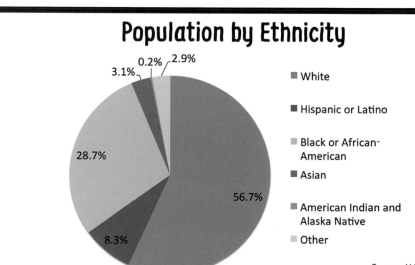

- White — 56.7%
- Hispanic or Latino — 8.3%
- Black or African-American — 28.7%
- Asian — 3.1%
- American Indian and Alaska Native — 0.2%
- Other — 2.9%

Source: U.S. Census Bureau.

Lover's Leap is located in Rock City, atop Lookout Mountain. It is said that from this point you can see seven states.

FAMOUS PEOPLE

Dr. Martin Luther King Jr. (1929–1968) was a civil rights leader. He helped get the Civil Rights Act of 1964 passed. King won the 1964 Nobel Peace Prize for leading nonviolent civil rights marches. He was born in Atlanta.

Jimmy Carter (1924–) was the 39th U.S. president (1977–1981). He also served as governor of Georgia (1971–1975) and won the 2002 Nobel Peace Prize. He was born in Plains.

Clarence Thomas (1948–) is a judge. In 1991 he became the second African-American appointed to the U.S. Supreme Court. He was born in Pin Point.

Julia Roberts (1967–) is an Academy award-winning movie actress. She has starred in many movies, including *Pretty Woman* (1990), *Erin Brockovich* (2000), *Eat, Pray, Love* (2010), and *August: Osage County* (2013). She was born in Smyrna.

Alice Walker (1944–) is a poet and novelist. Her books include *The Color Purple* (1982), which won the National Book Award and was later made into a movie. She was born in Eatonton.

Jackie Robinson (1919–1972) was the first African-American to play major league baseball. He was named to the National Baseball Hall of Fame in 1962. He was born in Cairo.

STATE SYMBOLS

Tree

live oak

Flower

Cherokee rose

Bird

brown thrasher

Reptile

gopher tortoise

PebbleGo Next Bonus! To make a dessert using Georgia's state fruit, go to www.pebblegonext.com and search keywords:

GA RECIPE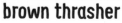

Marine Animal

right whale

Vegetable

Vidalia sweet onion

Crop

peanut

Fruit

peach

Fossil

shark tooth

Insect

honeybee

FAST FACTS

STATEHOOD
1788

CAPITAL ☆
Atlanta

LARGEST CITY •
Atlanta

SIZE
57,513 square miles (148,958 square kilometers) land area (2010 U.S. Census Bureau)

POPULATION
9,992,167 (2013 U.S. Census estimate)

STATE NICKNAME
Peach State

STATE MOTTO
"Wisdom, justice, and moderation"

STATE SEAL

The Great Seal of Georgia was adopted in 1799. The seal shows three pillars supporting an arch. The pillars represent the three branches of government. A man stands with a drawn sword. He is protecting the Constitution. A banner weaves through the pillars. The banner is printed with the state motto, "Wisdom, justice, and moderation." At the bottom is 1776, the date of the Declaration of Independence. The other side of the seal shows symbols of Georgia's trade and agriculture. A ship and a boat carry cotton and tobacco. A farmer plows a field as sheep graze nearby.

PebbleGo Next Bonus! To print and color your own flag, go to www.pebblegonext.com and search keywords:

GA FLAG

STATE FLAG

Georgia's state flag shows the state seal in gold on a field of blue. Thirteen white stars surround the seal. A gold ribbon is under the seal. The ribbon has small images of the three Georgia state flags from the past. It also has the current and first versions of the U.S. flag. Under the ribbon are the words "In God We Trust."

MINING PRODUCTS

kaolin and granite

MANUFACTURED GOODS

food products, chemicals, textiles, paper, transportation equipment, plastics and rubber products, machinery, computers and electronic equipment

FARM PRODUCTS

peanuts, chickens, eggs, tobacco, corn, cotton, soybeans, peaches

PROFESSIONAL SPORTS TEAMS

Atlanta Braves (MLB)
Atlanta Hawks (NBA)
Atlanta Dream (WNBA)
Atlanta Falcons (NFL)

PebbleGo Next Bonus! To learn the lyrics to the state song, go to www.pebblegonext.com and search keywords:

GA SONG

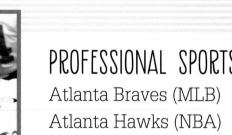

GEORGIA TIMELINE

1540 Spanish explorer Hernando de Soto is one of the first Europeans to arrive in Georgia.

1620 The Pilgrims establish a colony in the New World in present-day Massachusetts.

1732 King George II of England creates the Georgia colony.

1733 Englishman James Oglethorpe brings the first English settlers to Georgia and founds Savannah.

 **1777** Georgia's first state constitution is adopted.

 **1778** British troops capture Savannah during the Revolutionary War (1775–1783).

1788 Georgia becomes the 4th U.S. state on January 2.

 1838 The last of the Cherokee Indians are forced to leave Georgia and move west to Indian Territory. Thousands of Cherokee die during the journey, which is known as the Trail of Tears.

 1861 Georgia leaves the Union and joins the Confederacy.

 **1861–1865**

The Union and the Confederacy fight the Civil War. Georgia fights for the Confederacy. Many battles are fought in Georgia during the war.

 **1864**

Union troops led by General William T. Sherman attack Georgia. Sherman and his men capture Atlanta in September and Savannah in December.

1870

Georgia rejoins the Union after the Civil War.

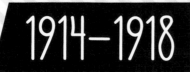 **1914–1918**

World War I is fought; the United States enters the war in 1917.

 **1920s** Insects called boll weevils destroy much of Georgia's cotton crops.

 **1939–1945** World War II is fought; the United States enters the war in 1941.

 **1960s** Dr. Martin Luther King Jr. leads the civil rights movement.

 **1976** Former Georgia governor Jimmy Carter is elected the 39th president of the United States.

 **1994** Floods in central and southern Georgia cause 31 deaths and millions of dollars in damages.

 **1996** Atlanta hosts the Summer Olympic Games.

 **2007–2009** Much of Georgia suffers a severe drought. To save water, people and businesses reduce the amount of water they use.

 **2014** Snow causes a major traffic jam in and around Atlanta on January 28, stranding motorists and students on school buses for hours.

2015 Georgia Aquarium hosts first Google Week; Google's sponsorship provided field trips for 3,600 students from the Atlanta area.

Glossary

artifact *(AR-tuh-fact)*—an object used in the past that was made by people

descendant *(di-SEN-duhnt)*—your descendants are your children, their children, and so on into the future

drought *(DROUT)*—a long period of weather with little or no rainfall

economy *(i-KAH-nuh-mee)*—the ways in which a country handles its money and resources

executive *(ig-ZE-kyuh-tiv)*—the branch of government that makes sure laws are followed

gallery *(GAL-uh-ree)*—a place where art is shown and sold

industry *(IN-duh-stree)*—a business which produces a product or provides a service

legislature *(LEJ-iss-lay-chur)*—a group of elected officials who have the power to make or change laws for a country or state

plateau *(pla-TOH)*—an area of high, flat land

poultry *(POHL-tree)*—farm birds raised for their eggs and meat

region *(REE-juhn)*—a large area

textile *(TEK-stile)*—a fabric or cloth that has been woven or knitted

Read More

Ganeri, Anita. *United States of America: A Benjamin Blog and His Inquisitive Dog Guide.* Country Guides. Chicago: Heinemann Raintree, 2015.

Haywood, Karen. *Georgia.* It's My State! New York: Marshall Cavendish, 2013.

Wang, Andrea. *What's Great About Georgia?* Our Great States. Minneapolis: Lerner Publications, 2014.

Internet Sites

FactHound offers a safe, fun way to find Internet sites related to this book. All of the sites on FactHound have been researched by our staff.

Here's all you do:

Visit *www.facthound.com*

Type in this code: 9781515703969

 Check out projects, games and lots more at
www.capstonekids.com

Critical Thinking Using the Common Core

1. What are Georgia's four largest cities? (Key Ideas and Details)

2. Georgia suffered a severe drought from 2007 to 2009. To save water, people and businesses reduced the amount of water they used. List a few ways you can save water throughout the day. (Integration of Knowledge and Ideas)

3. Textiles are among Georgia's top manufactured products. What are textiles? (Craft and Structure)

Index